THE HISTORY OF .NET WEB DEVELOPMENT

AND THE CORE THAT WAS NO MORE

IRIS CLASSON

ISBN: 978-91-987783-5-9

DEDICATION

I dedicate this book to my fellow programmers that are as confused as I am.

ACKNOWLEDGMENTS

To my family, thank you for putting up with me and all my writing.
To the community, thank you for the feedback and the support.

Who this book is for

This book is mainly for .NET software developers that would like to know more about the history of .NET web development. It doesn't matter if you've been programming for five minutes, five years or fifteen years, this book makes no assumptions and has no prerequisites.

What this book covers

Chapter 1

This chapter covers the timeline from when the internet was invented to approximately 2011. We will look at Classic ASP, ASP, ASP.NET, Web Forms, Silverlight, as well as ASP.NET MVC and Razor.

Chapter 2

This chapter focuses on server-to-server communication and covers the timeline from Dynamic Data Exchange, back in the good old days, to what we later got to know as Web API.

Chapter 3

This chapter is a short introduction to WinJS and TypeScript.

Chapter 4

This chapter covers the cross-platform problem.

Chapter 5

This chapter is dedicated to .NET Core and ASP.NET Core.

Chapter 6

This chapter is a continuation of the *Early Web Development* chapter. It ties everything together as we talk about ASP.NET Core, Razor, Razor Pages, and Blazor.

Chapter 7

This chapter discusses the end of .NET Core and .NET Standard.

Chapter 8

This chapter covers the last versions of ASP.NET and Blazor and discusses the future of .NET development.

Download color images

The images used in this book can also be found at:

https://historyofdotnetdevelopment/images/webdevelopment.xml

Alternatively, https://historyofdotnetdevelopment/images/webdevelopment.pdf

Errata / updates

For minor typos the book will keep its ISBN, however, big updates will be published as new versions with separate ISBNs. Contact me if you've purchased an older version and would like a discount for a later version (or a free eBook version).

If you've purchased the eBook, you should be able to download the latest version unless it's Kindle. AS above, contact me and I'll help you.
book@irisclasson.com

Errata can be found here: https://historyofdotnetdevelopment/errata.txt

Conventions used in this book

We used the following typographical conventions in this book:

Plain text indicates content.

Incline indicates quotes.

> *Incline with a left side border*
> indicates extra information that can be skipped.

`Sans serif text with gray background` indicates code example.

Preface

The .NET framework is a popular web development platform that enables developers to create robust, scalable applications. However, .NET is not just a single technology but rather a collection of technologies that work together to provide a comprehensive development platform. As a result, understanding the history of .NET development is essential for any developer who wants to use the platform effectively.

Easier said than done, I know.

I'll never forget the overwhelming feeling of not knowing anything during my freshman year. At the age of 27, a senior citizen in software developer years, I had decided to forgo my career as a licensed clinical dietitian and personal trainer to learn programming. How hard could it be? I spent the summer copy-pasting code from a book and StackOverflow, and with confidence high, I showed up on my first day of school feeling halfway there. Unsurprisingly, I was in for a big shock. There was a lot, and I mean A LOT, I had to learn, and I had no idea where to begin. The teachers had our backs, and by the end of the two-year degree, we were all confident programmers again, only to realize they had merely sheltered us from the harsh reality of programming.

You will never know it all, and sometimes the abundance of information online makes it even harder to make sense of it all, in particular, when it comes to timelines and releases.

Therefore, my mission with this book is to guide you through the .NET web development timeline. How to get from a to b to c, why b was killed and a was reinvented, and c made it big. I hope you enjoy reading this as much as I did writing it.

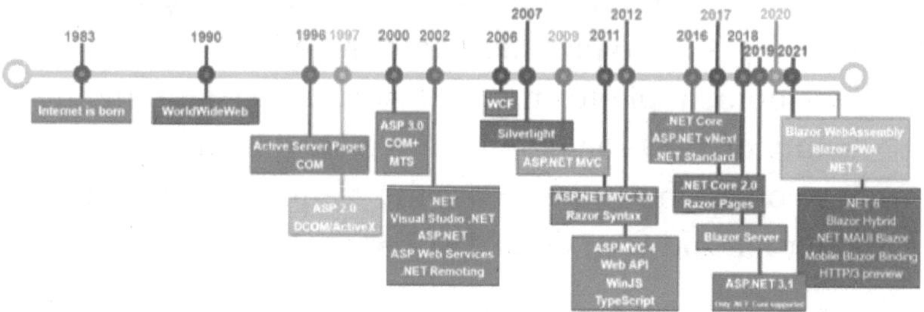

Figure 1.NET Web Development timeline. Larger image can be found in other chapters.

1

Early Web Development

The Internet

The internet was born out of a need for better communication. Little did we know it would become a human necessity that would fit right at the bottom of Maslow's Hierarchy of Needs.

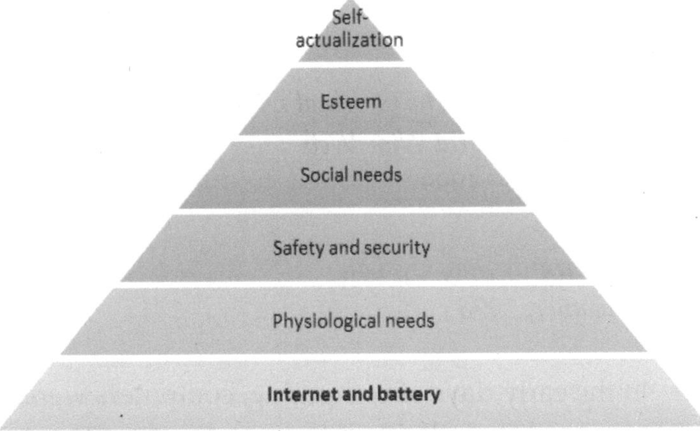

Figure 2 Maslow's Hierarchy of Needs with internet.

In today's world, the internet is a human necessity. It is an essential part of our daily lives, and we rely on it for everything from communication to entertainment. The internet has revolutionized the way we live and has made the world a smaller place. It has brought together people from all over the globe and has given us a platform to share our ideas and cultures. The internet is a powerful tool that can connect us with others and make our lives richer, and it's hard for many of us to imagine a life before the Internet was around.

I won't write too long about the history of the internet and the web, but if you'd like to read more about it, check out the note section below. *The Medium is the Massage* is not a spelling mistake, and although it's an old book, preceding the internet, it's a classic and a fascinating read.

Further reading

The Medium is the Massage
Marshall McLuhan, 1967

Weaving The Web: The Original Design and Ultimate Destiny of the World Wide Web
Tim Berners-Lee,1999

Where Wizards Stay Up Late
Katie Hafner, 1996

In the early days of computing, computers were largely used for individual tasks and were not connected to each other. However, as computing became more powerful and widespread, the need for networking emerged. The modern internet, as we know it today, was born in the early 1960s, with the development of packet-switching technology. This new way of transmitting data allowed computers to communicate with each other for the first time, laying the foundation for the global network we use today. In the 1970s, the first commercialized version of this packet-switching technology was introduced, followed by the development of the TCP/IP protocol in the 1980s. This protocol became the standard for how information is transmitted over the internet, and it is still in use today. With these new technologies, the internet took shape and grew into the vital tool it is today.

The official birthday of the Internet is January 1, 1983. Before this, computer networks didn't have a standard approach for interacting with one another. Each network had its own rules, which made it hard for different types of computers to talk to each other. The Defense Data Network (DDN) was the first Wide Area Network (WAN), which is a computer network that spans a large geographical area.

The DDN was born out of a need for the United States military to communicate with its computers around the world. For the DDN to work, all the different networks it comprised had to interact with each other. This led to the development of the Transmission Control Protocol/Internet Protocol (TCP/IP), which became the standard protocol for how information is transmitted over the internet. The TCP/IP protocol is still in use today, and it is what allows different types of computers to communicate with each other on the internet.

TCP/IP

> *TCP/IP is a set of communication protocols used to interconnect network devices on the Internet. TCP/IP includes four layers of protocols: the link layer, the internet layer, the transport layer, and the application layer. Each layer provides specific functions that enable devices to communicate with each other.*

The internet has come a long way since its humble beginnings in the early 1960s. What started as a small network of computers has grown into a global phenomenon, connecting people and machines all over the world. The development of new technologies has played a vital role in the growth of the internet, and software developers have played a vital part.

Early Web

The history of web development is a fascinating story of technological innovation and entrepreneurial ambition. The early days of the web saw a team of scientists at CERN develop the protocols for creating a global network of computers and in the years that followed, several companies and individuals played key roles in shaping the web as we know it today.

One of the most important figures was Tim Berners-Lee, who invented the World Wide Web in 1989. His book, *Weaving The Web: The Original Design and Ultimate Destiny of the World Wide Web*, was one of my book recommendations earlier.

Figure 3 Weaving The Web: The Original Design and Ultimate Destiny of the World Wide Web, Tim Berners-Lee

Tim Berners-Lee is often credited as the inventor of the World Wide Web. However, he prefers to think of himself as more of a "catalyzer" than an inventor. In the early 1990s, he saw the potential for a global system of interconnected documents that could be accessed by anyone with an Internet connection. However, he faced significant challenges in getting others to see the vision and adopt his technology. Undeterred, Berners-Lee persevered, and his tireless efforts eventually paid off.

Since then, the web has grown exponentially, with billions of people now using it for everything from communication to entertainment. The story of web development is one of constant evolution, and it seems certain that the next few years will bring even more exciting changes.

The first web browser was invented in 1990, also by Tim Berners-Lee. He called it "WorldWideWeb", and it was later renamed Nexus.

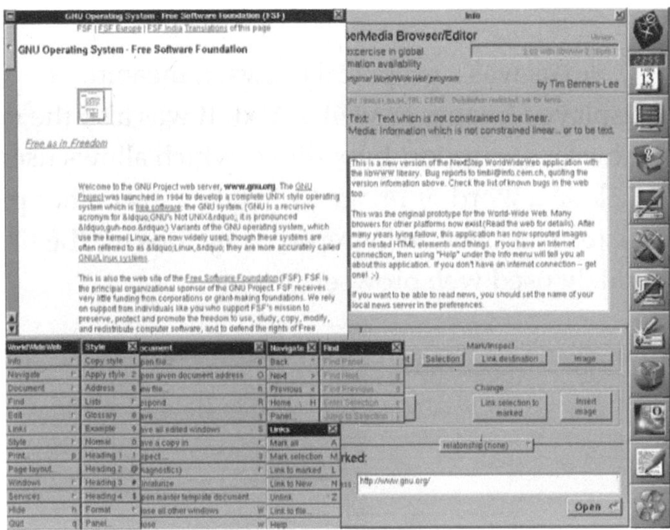

Figure 4 WorldWideWeb, 1994

Nexus was a graphical browser, meaning it displayed images as well as text. It was also the first browser to support hyperlinks, which allows users to click on a word or image to be taken to another page. Nexus was eventually replaced by Mosaic, the first widely used web browser.

Figure 5 Mosaic (image from NCSA)

Today, there are many web browsers available, each with its own unique features. However, they all trace their origins back to Tim Berners-Lee's original invention.

The popularity of the web increased rapidly thereafter, and by 1995, there were an estimated 10 million web users. Today, the web is an essential part of everyday life for billions of people around the globe and workplace for many web developers like me. I started doing web development not long before static websites became popular again after being shunned after the popularity of dynamic sites.

However, in the early years of the web, there were only a handful of websites, and the vast majority of these were static. This meant they only contained HTML files that were manually created and updated. There was no way to generate or update content dynamically on a website. But Perl, a scripting language, changed that.

Figure 6 Perl

Perl was created in 1987 by Larry Wall, and in the late 1990s, we saw the rise of Perl 5 as a CGI scripting language, in part due to its strong regular expression and string parsing capabilities. Perl quickly became the most popular server-side scripting language on the Web. Besides making it possible to create dynamic web pages, Perl has also had a profound impact on the way the Internet was used. For example, Perl was used to create the first web-based chat application, and it was used to create the first web-based email application.

As the popularity of the Web grew, so did the need for more powerful and reliable server-side scripting languages. With Perl, web developers could write scripts that generated HTML files on the fly. This made it possible to create dynamic websites, and Microsoft wasn't far behind.

Active Server Pages

In 1996, the first version of Active Server Pages (ASP) was released. ASP was a Microsoft technology that allowed developers to embed Perl code in HTML files. This made it possible to create dynamic websites using Microsoft's IIS web server.

Figure 7 Classic ASP (Active Server Pages) was the first server-side script engine created by Microsoft.

Active Server Pages (ASP) quickly gained popularity after its release. Many developers were attracted to the platform because of its ease of use and flexibility, and it quickly became a standard for building dynamic web applications. It was a simple-to-use server-side technology that revolutionized the web. ASP was designed as a set of objects with built-in capabilities for quickly and easily accessing common services supplied by the web server for the Internet.

It came pre-installed with Microsoft's Internet Information Services (IIS) web-server and required no additional action or configuration. It would work just as well as IIS, which is to say, it would operate out of the box. There were no browser-compatibility concerns, and browser plug-ins weren't required. It just worked well and allowed web developers to write scripts and create dynamic content.

I don't know how long you've been around, but if you were there when Classic ASP was still around, then I applaud you for being a part of that glorious time that marked the start of what would become one of the most popular web development frameworks.

Classic ASP was very similar to PHP in the sense it allowed you to mix your HTML with server-side script written in PerlScript, VBScript, or JScript. The code would then be interpreted and executed on the server before being returned to the browser as plain HTML. PHP, a server scripting language, was created by Rasmus Lerdorf in 1994, and its first implementation was in 1995. PHP is derived from the Personal Home Page (PHP) system, which was designed for use with web files. The name PHP is a recursive acronym for "PHP: Hypertext Preprocessor".

PHP, Perl, and ASP were the main technologies/languages used to create dynamic and interactive websites and are still around today, albeit after undergoing a lot of changes. Although ASP wasn't language per se (but a technology that let you leverage other languages such as the ones I mentioned earlier), many referred to it as a programming language due to its flexibility and feature richness.

Here is how one would print out the current time to the client:

```
// Server side

The server's current time:
<%
Response.Write Now()
%>
```

```
// Client side

The server's current time:
8/11/2015 6:24:45 PM
```

It was a big deal when it came out, as it was considered an important part of the next big step in modern computing- distributed computing. ASP could access data, build a model, do computing and business logic, and then dynamically generate HTML supported by any browser.

While Classic ASP was a great starting point, it had its limitations. The biggest one was that it was difficult to maintain and use for scale large applications. These were issued that led to further development and improvement of the framework.

ASP Versions

ASP 1.0 came out in 1996 as a part of IIS 3.0, and two more versions came before it was superseded ASP.NET in 2002.

> ***ASP releases***
> *ASP 1.0, December 1996 as part of IIS 3.0*
> *ASP 2.0, September 1997 as part of IIS 4.0*
> *ASP 3.0, November 2000 as part of IIS 5.0*

ASP.NET would not be possible without introducing the .NET Framework in 2002, which was a complete re-write of Microsoft's web development platform. It was released with Visual Studio .NET, another key milestone.

Visual Studio .NET and the .NET Framework

The release of Visual Studio .NET in 2002 signaled a major shift in the world of software development. For the first time, developers had a comprehensive toolset that enabled them to build applications for the Microsoft .NET Framework.

Figure 8 Visual Studio .NET Professional, 2002

This allowed developers to take advantage of the many benefits the .NET platform offered, including increased security, reliability, and scalability. In addition, Visual Studio .NET made it easier for developers to create applications that could be deployed across a wide range of devices and platforms. The release of Visual Studio .NET was a major milestone in the history of software development.

The same goes for the .NET Framework. It included a large class library called the Framework Class Library

(FCL) and a runtime environment called the Common Language Runtime (CLR).

.NET Main Components

The .NET Framework had four main components:
1. Common Language Runtime (CLR)
2. Framework Class Library (FCL),
3. Core Languages (WinForms, ASP.NET, and ADO.NET),
4. Other Modules (WCF, WPF, WF, Card Space, LINQ, Entity Framework, Parallel LINQ, Task Parallel Library, and more)

The CLR provided several benefits, including memory management, security, and exception handling. The FCL provided a wide range of functionality, from data access to graphical user interfaces. Microsoft .NET also supported multiple programming languages, making it easier for developers to create software for the platform.

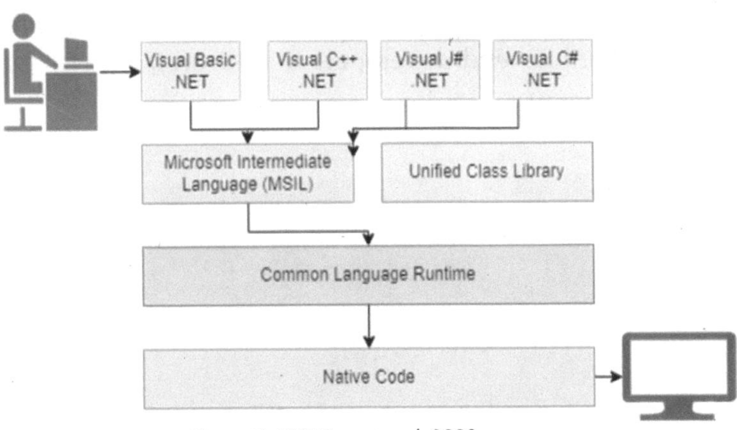

Figure 9 .NET Framework 2002

ASP.NET

When .NET was first released, it was widely seen as a major step forward for the software industry as it made it easier for developers to create software that was more reliable and easier to maintain.

This made ASP.NET more appealing to developers coming from different backgrounds, and although we didn't know it back then, this would be a key selling point for the framework in the years to come.

ASP.NET was an extended technology to the earlier classic ASP, but with the major difference it supported the .NET framework and let developers create user interfaces with Web Forms. Targeting the .NET framework meant you could choose any language as long as it supported the .NET framework, and the custom user interface classes meant you could use an object-oriented approach to building user interfaces, at least to some degree. You didn't have to learn complex syntaxes or a new language, and Web Forms made it easier for backend developers to take on front-end development.

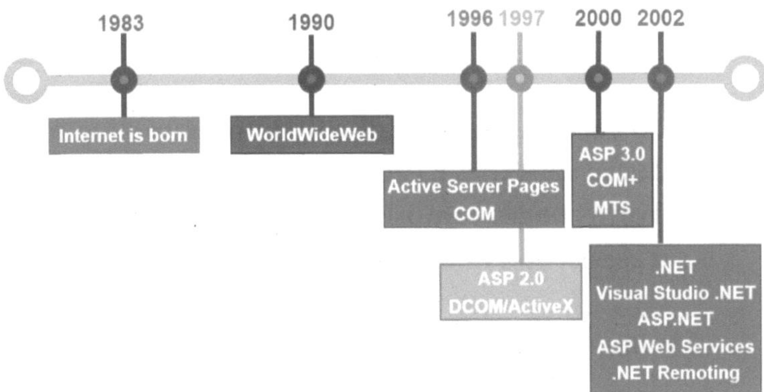

Figure 10 Early web development. Full timeline can be found at the end of this book.

Web Forms

Web Forms was one of the first programming models introduced in ASP.NET for creating web applications. Web Forms pages comprised two files, one for the visual aspect and one for the code.

Front-end example:

```
<!-- HelloCodebehind.aspx -->
<%@ Page Language="VB#"
Src="HelloCodebehind.aspx.vb"
Inherits= MyWebPage %>
<HTML>
   <HEAD>   </HEAD>
<BODY>
<FORM RUNAT="SERVER">YOUR NAME: 
<asp:textbox id=txtName
Runat="server"></asp:textbox>
<p><asp:button id=cmdEcho
onclick=cmdEcho_Click Text="Echo"
   runat="server" tooltip="Click to echo
your name"></asp:button></p>
<asp:label id=lblGreeting
runat="server"></asp:label>
</FORM>
</BODY>
</HTML>
```

Code-behind file in VB:

```
' HelloCodebehind.aspx.vb
Imports System
Imports System.Web
Imports System.Web.UI
Imports System.Web.UI.WebControls

Public Class MyWebPage
       Inherits System.Web.UI.Page
       Protected txtName As TextBox
       Protected cmdEcho As Button
       Protected lblGreeting As Label
       Protected Sub cmdEcho_Click(Source As
Object, _e As EventArgs)
            lblGreeting.Text="Hello, " &
txtName.Text
       End Sub
End Class
```

Web Forms was a component-oriented framework that had a high concept of compatibility with Windows Forms, the framework used for desktop application development.

It provided an event-driven model that desktop developers were familiar with. It made it easier to transition from desktop development to web development. Visual Studio provided a rich toolset and support for third party toolsets, with familiar controls, such as buttons, input fields, and more. Both Web Forms and Windows Forms (the desktop equivalent) applications were typically built using a drag-and-drop approach, where designers could create pages by dragging controls from a toolbox. The drag-and-drop approach was simple and easy to use, but it resulted in pages that were often very heavy with a lot of code behind them. Web Forms gained a lot of popularity and remained the predominant approach to web development for many years.

I used to work for a component vendor, named Telerik, and although we had component kits for a wide range of platforms, from Web Forms on the Web to MVC on Windows Phone and even Windows Mobile, Web Forms was always the most popular component kit we sold.

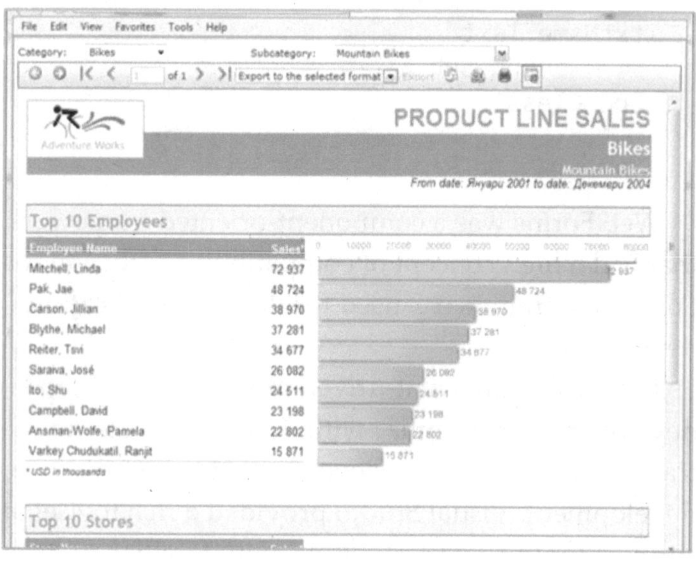

Figure 11 Telerik components from back in the days

The event-driven approach made it easy to put together a web application fast. Additionally, it offered familiarity. This was however at the expense of fine-grained control, testability, and extensibility. Thus, in 2007, Microsoft announced they were working on another programming model, ASP.NET MVC.

Before we continue with ASP.NET MVC, let's talk about another release. 2007 was a busy year full of exciting surprises for .NET developers. Several important announcements for .NET developers were made, and one of them was a new project Scott Guthrie (Microsoft) had been working on, Silverlight.

Where did Silverlight fit in, in all this?

Silverlight

In the early 1990s Macromedia acquired FutureSplash and rebranded it to what we later came to know as Flash. Flash was a two-part system, a graphics and animation editor known as Macromedia Flash, and a media player known as Macromedia Flash Player.

Figure 12 Adobe Flash logo

The Flash Player was a web browser plugin that could run the SWF files created in the Flash authoring tool. Macromedia was later acquired by Adobe, in 2005, and it quickly became the defacto tool for creating vector graphics and animations for the web. Microsoft was quick to create a contender, and few were surprised when Scott Guthrie announced Silverlight, a "cross platform, cross browser .NET plug-in that enables designers and developers to build rich media experiences and RIAs for browsers."

Figure 13 Microsoft Silverlight

Silverlight, released in 2007, provided a Flash-like runtime environment for browser-based, cross-platform applications and streaming media content. In other words, it was designed to be an alternative to Adobe Flash Player. Its popularity grew fast, with an impressive adoption rate. It was used to power some of the most popular applications on the web, including Netflix, Hulu, and Amazon Prime Video. Silverlight had also been used to create interactive experiences for a variety of brands, including Coca-Cola, Nissan, and NBC Sports. However, in 2011, industry experts predicted the death of Silverlight and Flash (later) due to HTML5. Two years later, Microsoft announced that Silverlight would be discontinued.

> ***Silverlight releases***
>
> *v1.* 2007*
> *v2.* 2008*
> *v3.* 2009*
> *v4.* 2010*
> *v5.* 2011*
> *Last v5 build release: 2019*

ASP.NET MVC

Two years, in 2009, after the initial Silverlight release, the first official version of ASP.NET MVC was released. It followed the Mode-View-Controller pattern, which added separation of concerns, a pattern that was very popular at the time. Ruby on Rails, a similar framework (but for Ruby), was said to be an inspiration. And although I don't know if that is true, I do remember the many heated discussions regarding which was better, as many were quick to notice the similarities.

"Microsoft launched ASP.NET MVC 1.0 at the MIX09 event last month. This new ASP.NET enhancement brings a Rails-like model-view-controller framework to Microsoft's Web development stack." - Arstechnica, RYAN PAUL - 4/3/200

> ***Ruby on Rails***

> *Ruby on Rails is a web application framework written in the Ruby programming language. It makes programming web applications easier by making assumptions about what every developer needs to get started. It included everything needed to create a database-backed web application, using the Model-View-Controller (MVC) pattern.*

The idea to separate the logic, driven by the increasingly complex websites, came from the MVC pattern. The Model-View-Controller (MVC) pattern is a way of organizing code so different parts of the application are responsible for different tasks. The Model is responsible for the data, the View is responsible for the presentation and would be written with Razor or ASPX syntax, and the Controller would be responsible for the logic.

The Model-View-Controller (MVC) separation made it possible to develop advanced graphical user interfaces (GUIs) that could be updated independently of the underlying data models. Just as important, developers could create sophisticated applications without spaghetti code.

ASP.NET MVC was open sourced a week later under a Microsoft Public License (MS-PL). The adoption rate was impressive, and Microsoft churned out new features every year. The table below sums up some for the features for each release.

Version	Released	Features (some)
MVC 1.0	2009	• MVC architecture

		• Routing • HTML and Ajax Helpers
MVC 2.0	2010	• Areas • Async controller • Client-side validation • Custom template • Scaffolding
MVC 3.0	2011	• Razor view engine • Global filters • ViewBag
MVC 4.0	2012	• Mobile template • Bundling, minification • Windows Azure SDK • Web API
MVC 5.0	2013	• Authentication filters • Bootstrap • ASP.Net Identity
MVC 5.2	2014	• Attribute based routing

Silverlight had never been a competitor to ASP.NET MVC, and in fact, the two technologies were complementary. MVC allowed developers to create rich applications using well-established design patterns, while Silverlight provided a powerful platform for delivering Flash-like content. With Microsoft's move away from Silverlight, many developers began to wonder if they should continue to invest in MVC or make the switch to another framework. However, Microsoft's continuous investment in ASP.NET convinced developers to stay, and a big change was right around the corner.

Razor

In 2011, with the 3rd MVC release, a new syntax was introduced, Razor.

Razor was a templating view engine that used a new syntax, Razor, which was an improved markup syntax for the views. It allowed for much cleaner code, and it was easier to read. The downside was a step away from the drag-and-drop in Web Forms that many backend developers had embraced. However, the general consensus was that it was a step in the right direction, and front-end wasn't a foreign idea anymore.

Razor replaced the ASPX markup we looked at earlier. Instead of two files, one for the front end/client and a code-behind file that would output to the client, there was one file, and you'd use a specific syntax to bake in C# code. Sound familiar? Yes, it was like Classic ASP (and in the first release even slower than Classic ASP), as many pointed out. But there was one big difference, and that was, while Classic ASP had the business logic in the same file rendered to the end user, Razor syntax was used for the view logic only, not business logic.

Here is a comparison:

```
// aspx

<h1>ASPX example</h1>
<h3>
    Hello <%=name%>
</h3>
<p>
    Visit <a href="/About/<%=product%>"> our
product page</a>
</p>
```

```
// razor

<h1>Razor example</h1>
<h3>
    Hello @name>
</h3>
<p>
    Visit <a href="/About/@product>"> our
product page</a>
</p>
```

ASP.NET had, in just a few years, evolved and become a feature rich framework for web development. However, a lot was also happening in terms of server-to-server communication, with the 4.0 release of ASP.NET MVC ASP.NET Web API.

Let's take a look at how we got there, and why that was a significant release.

2

DCOM, WCF AND WEB API

Let's take a step back to early 2000. As systems were growing and becoming more complex, the need for web services grew. Distributed systems needed ways to communicate with each other, with different clients, across operating systems and languages. Business to business transactions and feature components became more common, and at the same time, decoupling and independent scaling became a core need for distributed systems. Over a short period of time, we had gone from specialized and isolated components to cross-domain systems with a complexity we couldn't even dream of a decade earlier.

Dynamic Data Exchange (DDE)

In 1987, Microsoft introduced one of their first inter-process communication methods, DDE – Dynamic Data Exchange, that had a publish-subscribe model. A program subscribed to changes and was notified when a change happened.

Figure 14 .Pub-sub model

On top of DDE, and somewhat superseding DDE, was OLE – Object Linking and Embedding. OLE was object based, and when OLE 2.0 was released in 1993, COM was the underlying object model. Component Object Model was a way to bundle business logic in reusable components, but this was limited to local work.

Distributed Common Object Model (DCOM)

The solution to COM's limitations was DCOM, Distributed Common Object Model. DCOM allowed communication between components on remote computers.

DCOM used Remote Procedure Calls, RPC, a request-response protocol designed to facilitate communication in a client-server manner irrespective of whether the communication was local or remote.

RPC allowed different machines to communicate with each other by invoking remote procedures. The RPC protocol was originally designed for use in UNIX operating systems. It was a simple and efficient way to communicate between different machines. It had a small footprint and could be easily implemented in any programming language. However, in later years, REST, representational state transfer, became more popular. We will talk about REST later. At the time of writing, RPC has made a strong comeback after being shunned for years, but that's a story for another book.

DCOM wasn't the only standardized RPC system out there. A big competitor was CORBA, another distributed component middleware that had steadily gained popularity since its release in 1990, 6 years before DCOM.

CORBA

CORBA was created in the late 1980s to enable distributed components to communicate with each other. The initial version of CORBA was based on the Common Object Request Broker Architecture (CORBA), which was developed by the Object Management Group (OMG). CORBA provided a standard way for components to interact, regardless of the programming language or operating system they were running on. To achieve this, CORBA defined several standards, including the IIOP protocol and the IDL language.

.NET Remoting

With the release of .NET in late 2000, .NET Remoting came to replace DCOM. .NET Remoting was a technology used for communication between application processes. It allowed an object in one process to interact with an object in another process, even if those objects were on different computers. .NET Remoting used a client-server model, in which the server provided access to objects, and the client invoked methods on those objects. It also supported different transportation protocols and serialization formats.

There were now several options in terms of distributed components middleware, but they all had limitations. Scaling was difficult, they were complex and often tied to specific platforms. An example would be .NET Remoting. It was Microsoft only and worked with binary or XML serialized objects. At the same time, web applications were changing and were doing more than just serving up pages. The nature and scope of distributed applications were changing. That inspired the creation of ASP Web Services in 2001, released in 2002.

ASP Web Services

With ASP Web Services, the aim was human readable messages based on open standards that would work across platforms- and just as important- simplicity.

ASP Web Services were a feature of the ASP.NET framework that allowed developers to create web services that could be consumed by other applications. These web services could be written in any .NET language, and they were deployed to a server where they could be accessed by clients over the internet. ASP Web Services used the Simple Object Access Protocol (SOAP) protocol to communicate with clients, and they could be invoked via HTTP GET and POST requests.

SOAP

SOAP is an acronym for "Simple Object Access Protocol". It is a messaging protocol that allows programs to communicate with each other over a network. SOAP messages are written in XML, and they consist of a message envelope, a message header, and a message body. The message envelope contains information about the sender and the recipient of the message. The message header contains information about the message, such as the encoding, the scheme, and the method. The message body contains the actual content of the message. SOAP messages are exchanged between two programs using a transport protocol, such as HTTP or SMTP.

In addition, ASP Web Services supported the WSDL standard, which allowed clients to generate code automatically that can be used to access the web service. As a result, ASP Web Services provided an easy way for developers to create and deploy web services that can be consumed by a wide range of clients.

Example:

```
  <%@ WebService language="C"
class="MyService" %>

  using System;
  using System.Web.Services;
  using System.Xml.Serialization;


[WebService(Namespace="http://localhost/MyWe
bServices/")]
  public class MyService : WebService
  {
      [WebMethod]
      public int Add(int a, int b)
      {
          return a + b;
      }

      [WebMethod]
      public String SayHello()
      {
          return "Hello World";
      }
  }
```

ASP Web Services supported several standards, such a as WSDL, HTTP and SOAP.

> *WSDL*
>
> *The Web Services Description Language (WSDL) is a standard format for describing a web service. It is typically used to provide machine-readable information about the web service, such as the types of data that can be passed to the service, the methods that can be called, and the format of the data that will be returned. WSDL can be used to generate client code automatically for accessing the web service, making it an essential tool for developers who want to consume web services. While WSDL is primarily intended for describing SOAP-based web services, it can also be used to describe RESTful web services.*

This meant that, as a consumer of a Web Service, you wouldn't need to know how the service was implemented, be that object model or language, as long as you as the consumer could read and use the same standards. Developers now had many options for communicating between processes, locally or remote. Across the internet with a service on a different platform, one would use Web Services, but for fast binary communication, you would probably use .NET Remoting and so on. A large system would often tie together components using different methods, increasing the complexity of the system. Windows Communication Foundation, unveiled in 2003 and released in 2006, was introduced to solve all this.

Windows Communication Foundation (WCF)

WCF was intended to be a unified programming model for building service-oriented applications with explicit support for service-oriented development. It enabled developers to create secure and reliable services that could be consumed by a wide range of clients, including web browsers, mobile devices, and traditional rich clients. WCF services could be accessed using a variety of protocols, including HTTP, HTTPS, TCP, and MSMQ. WCF also provided support for duplex messaging, which allowed clients and servers to communicate with each other asynchronously.

A WCF application consisted of three components: a service, host, and service client. Here is a simple example of the service contract declaration and the config file.

```
// Interface using WCF
using System.ServiceModel;

[ServiceContract]
interface IGreeting
{
 [OperationContract]

 string SayHello(String name);
}
```

```
//web.config for WCF Service
<?xml version="1.0" encoding="utf-8"?>
<configuration

xmlns="http://schemas.microsoft.com/.NetConf
iguration/v2.0">
   <system.serviceModel>
      <services>
         <service
serviceType="SelfHostedService.Greeting">
            <endpoint
address="http://localhost:8080/greeting"

bindingSectionName="basicProfileBinding"

contractType="SelfHostedService.IGreeting"/>

         </service>
      </services>
   </system.serviceModel>
</configuration>
```

Windows Communication Foundation differed a lot from ASP Web Services. Here are other major differences:

WCF supported a range of protocols: HTTP, Named Pipes, TCP, and more. Web service was limited to HTTP protocol.

WCF supported several types of bindings, such as BasicHttpBinding, WSDualHttpBinding, WSHttpBinding, etc., while a web service supported only SOAP or XML.

It had different hosting options (Windows Service, IIS, Windows Activation Service) while web services could only by hosted by IIS.

Additionally, WCF had features web services didn't have, such as extended security features, better serialization, improved exception handling, multi-threading, and more.

REST

I mentioned RPC earlier, but I didn't talk about REST (Representational State Transfer). REST was considered a lightweight alternative to RPC and SOAP, and it quickly became a buzzword after being introduced by Roy Fielding in his dissertation in 2000.

Figure 15 A RESTful API

REST, or Representational State Transfer, is a popular architectural style for building web services. RESTful web services provide a way to access and manipulate data over the HTTP protocol. To be truly RESTful, a web service must adhere to several constraints, such as being stateless and having a well-defined interface. However, these constraints also make RESTful web services easy to use and scalable. As a result, REST has become a popular choice for building web services that need to handle numerous requests. RESTful systems provide a consistent interface for clients and servers, making it easy to build scalable and maintainable applications. REST has become the de facto standard for building web APIs, and many popular web services are based on the REST architecture. However, REST is not limited to the web; it can be used to design distributed systems of any kind. With its simple and elegant design, REST has revolutionized how we build distributed applications.

Around the time WCF popularity peaked, the interest in REST APIs grew and soon the majority of APIs were REST APIs. Consequentially, developers kept pushing for REST over SOAP.

Ironically, few seem to agree on what exactly REST is, and even fewer have read his dissertation. Nonetheless, developers wanted REST, and WCF provided some support for REST-style services. But it still had some limitations. The WCF Web API project was intended to fill the gaps and eventually evolved and became what we later got to know as Web API.

WEB API

The ASP.NET Web API was an extensible framework for building HTTP based services that could be accessed in different applications on different platforms, such as web, windows, mobile, etc. It worked more or less the same way as ASP.NET MVC web applications, except it sent data as a response instead of html view. It was similar to WCF services, but the exception was that it only supported the HTTP protocol, which was gaining in popularity over the alternatives.

Overall, one could say Microsoft created Web API to provide developers with more flexibility, as well as simplicity.

Web API was released with ASP.NET MVC 4.0 in 2012. Although Web API quickly became the de facto framework for HTTP based services, Microsoft was careful not to rule out WCF. They received a lot of criticism for this, but at the time of writing, the trends have shifted again, and I can sympathize with their reluctance to rule out other technologies.

To quote Microsoft:

"Although WCF provides some support for writing REST-style services, the support for REST in ASP.NET Web API is more complete and all future REST feature improvements will be made in ASP.NET Web API."

It's important to understand that Web API was a framework for developing RESTful HTTP services. It was not intended to replace WCF and wasn't the only way to create and expose an API.

Web API was quickly embraced, partly because it tied in nicely with the ASP.NET MVC style of programming.

Web API vs ASP.NET MVC

Both ASP.NET MVC and ASP.NET Web API followed the Model, View, Controller pattern with actions defined in the controllers. The actions followed a REST inspired model. This was in contrast to, for example, Web Forms, which was largely event driven like we talked about earlier. The distinction between ASP.NET MVC and Web API was less clear. The main difference was that ASP.NET MVC used a web engine to render web pages dynamically, as it predominately was designed to create standard web applications, while Web API was designed to create RESTful/HTTP applications. Web API had a logical layer for content negotiation. Content negotiation lets the client and server negotiate so the best available data format can be used. Content negotiation could be implemented in ASP.NET MVC, but what would be harder to implement was the lack of dependency on IIS.

But where did ASP.NET Core fit in? Let's talk about .NET Core and ASP.NET Core.

3

WinJS and TypeScript

WinJS, Windows Library for JavaScript, was released (at the time only for Windows Store Applications) with Windows 8 in 2011/2012. WinJS provided a set of JavaScript controls and templates that could be used in a Windows Store application (later rebranded to Universal Windows Applications). The goal of WinJS was to provide a set of HTML/CSS controls with a consistent look and feel and to reach out to front-end developers. WinJS was later changed to be used in browsers and open sourced.

Soon after WinJS, in 2012, TypeScript, a language that is a syntactical superset of JavaScript, was announced and open sourced from the start. When I wrote this section, I wasn't sure which chapter was the best fit, but I think it makes sense as an introduction to TypeScript. For many, WinJS was an introduction to TypeScript.

```
(function () {

    "use strict";

    var app = WinJS.Application;

    var activation =
Windows.ApplicationModel.Activation;

    WinJS.strictProcessing();

    app.onactivated = function (args) {

        if (args.detail.kind ===
activation.ActivationKind.launch) {

            if
(args.detail.previousExecutionState !==
activation.ApplicationExecutionState.termina
ted) {
                // TODO: App launch
            } else {

                // TODO: App suspension
            }
args.setPromise(WinJS.UI.processAll());
        }
    };
    app.oncheckpoint = function (args) {
        // TODO: App soon suspended
    };
    app.start();
})();
```

Figure 16 WinJS example. Empty app.

At least it was for me. At the same time, both of them signaled a change in Microsoft's mindset regarding Open Source, a shift that would later change the .NET.

I was all about Windows Store Apps, which at the inception was called Metro Apps, so much so, I wrote a book about them and how to create Metro Apps. I was still at Telerik in component heaven as a Technical Evangelist, and WinJS was one of the few things that made me want to work with JavaScript. Like other developers, I had tried my fair share of JavaScript replacements and supersets, desperate to avoid using plain JavaScript with its long list of problems. While many disappeared just as fast as they were created, TypeScript gained traction and made it big.

The language was developed to provide a more reliable and flexible scripting language for large-scale applications. Typescript became increasingly popular over the years, and it is now used by many major organizations, including Google, Facebook, and Amazon. While Typescript is not yet as widely used as JavaScript, its popularity grew rapidly, and it will likely become the standard scripting language for large-scale web applications.

With TypeScript, it was clear that Microsoft was making a shift towards open source with a new and refreshing developer focus, as well as embracing other platforms. Change was in the air.

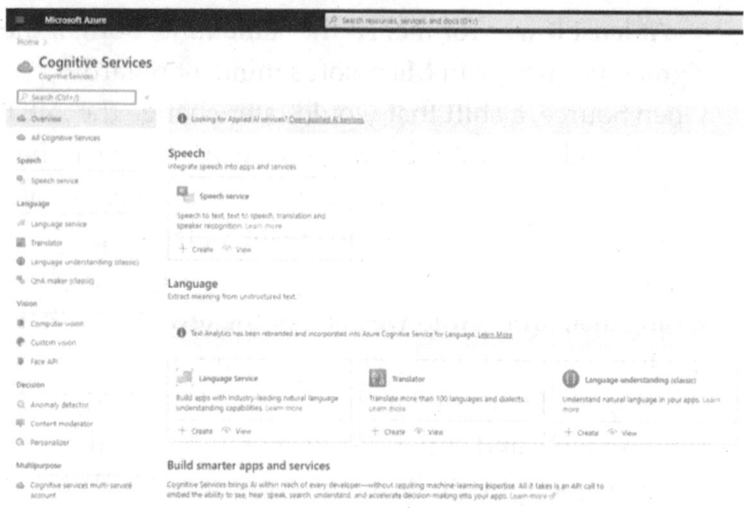

Figure 17 The Azure portal was written in TypeScript

4

Cross platform dreams

NET subsets and Portable Class Libraries

Ironically, the many groundbreaking releases Microsoft made over the years also caused a problem with the many subsets of the .NET framework. Such as .NET Compact Framework, Silverlight, Windows Phone, Windows Store, and so on. They were maintained independently, and what they had in common was somewhat by coincidence or by sharing similar starting points. Creating libraries that spawned the different subsets was a pain. I remember battling with linked files and preprocessor compilation symbols and builds, while still having to resort to separate libraries for some functionality. The problems with linked files were many. It was easy to forget where the file originally was and inadvertently making a change that wasn't tested in other projects. The link would break, Intellisense would randomly stop working, and there were many other problems that were later addressed.

Intellisense

IntelliSense is a code completion tool that makes it easier to write code in Visual Studio. When you type code, IntelliSense displays a list of suggested symbols you can use to complete the code statement. IntelliSense also provides information about the symbol, such as its type or signature. This information can help you choose the correct symbol when writing code. IntelliSense is available for many languages, including C#, Visual Basic, and JavaScript. You can customize IntelliSense to match your development style.

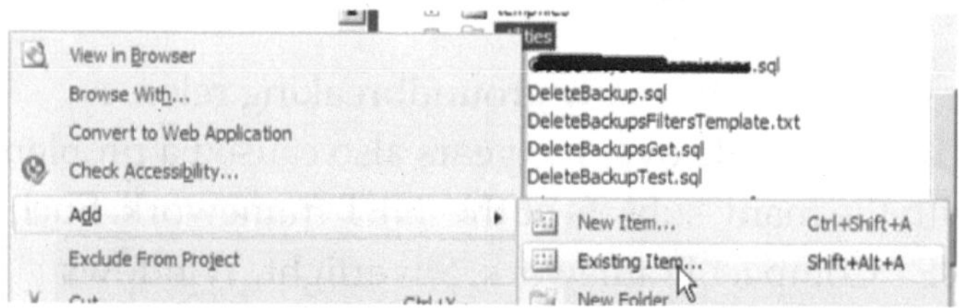

Figure 18 Adding linked files was a multi-step process

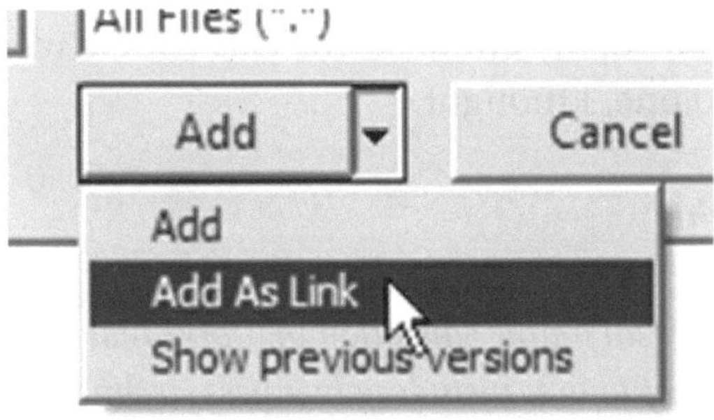

Figure 19 One could also add files in the .csproj file instead, but through the UI was easier

When portable libraries came out, I got my hopes up and quickly became a fan and advocate. But they weren't as portable as the name indicated. Portable class libraries looked at the targeted platforms and found the common ground, and that became the boundaries for what you could use.

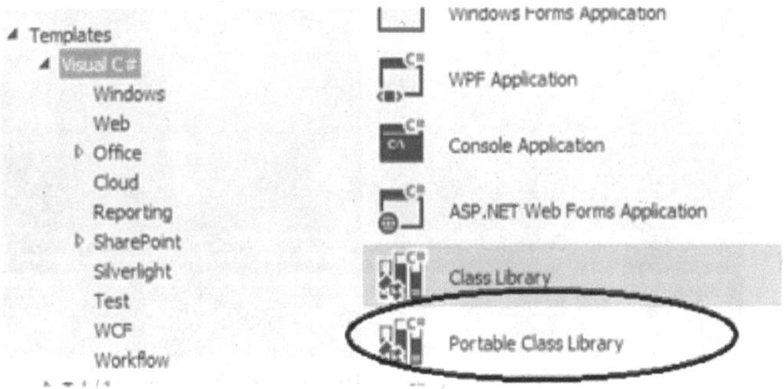

Figure 20 Portable Class Libraries just suddenly appeared as an option one day

If I targeted Windows Phone and Xbox, then only libraries that supported both were available to me. And that wasn't much. But I was confident this was the new golden standard and the solution we had waited for, so I went in head-first and even created a Pluralsight course, sharing my enthusiasm. This course will be a long-lived one, I thought.

Pluralsight

Pluralsight is an online education platform that offers courses on a variety of topics, including business, technology, and creative arts. The company was founded in 2004 by Aaron Rasmussen and Scott Dinsmore, and it has since grown to become one of the largest providers of online learning content. Pluralsight offers both subscription-based and pay-per-course options, and it has a team of over 1,000 expert instructors. Besides its comprehensive course catalog, Pluralsight offers certification prep materials and corporate training solutions.

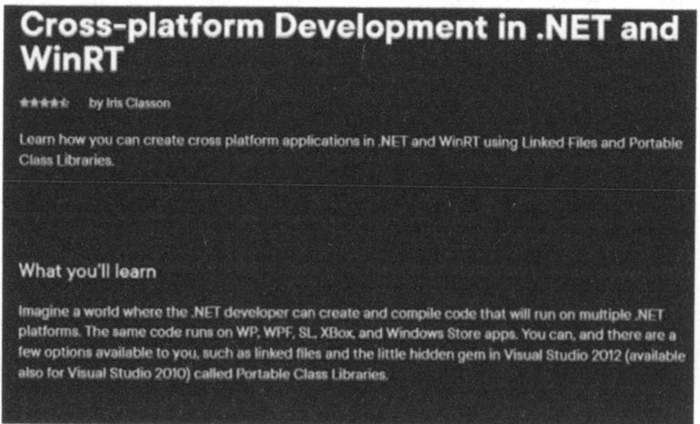

Figure 21 A Pluralsight course

Well, it wasn't. Portable Class Libraries didn't solve all the problems; it created new ones. Linked files still were the preferred option for many (but not for me). Of course, I also added a section about linked files that in my course, but with less enthusiasm.

Many problems I mentioned earlier contributed to the motivation to build .NET Core and later the .NET Standard.

5

.NET Core and ASP.NET Core

.NET Core and ASP.NET vNEXT

2014 was the year many exciting announcements were made by Microsoft.

Microsoft's announcement of ASP.NET vNext and .NET Core at their BUILD conference in San Francisco in 2014 (released in 2016) came as a surprise to many in the developer community. While the news were widely welcomed, there was also some confusion about what these new technologies entailed.

Together, these two technologies represented a major shift in Microsoft's development platform strategy, and they had the potential to simplify the process of building modern web applications.

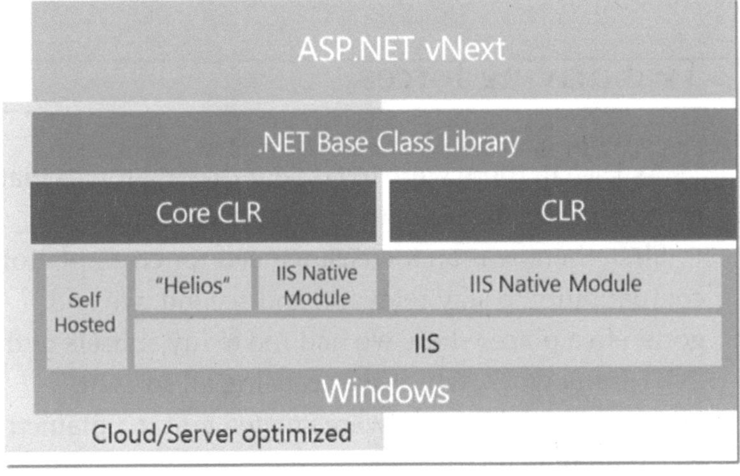

Figure 22 ASP.NET vNext was later known as ASP.NET Core

ASP.NET Core was a complete rewrite of ASP.NET and was later known as ASP.NET 5 (and by some as project K), until Microsoft realized the name was confusing and renamed it ASP.NET Core. .NET Core was first announced as .NET Core 5, but since developers wondered where on earth the 1st, 2nd ,3rd and 4th releases were (there weren't any), they renamed it to .NET Core 1.0, which made sense. .NET Core was a new concept, even if it built on old ideas. Unfortunately, with ASP.NET Core, the confusion remained. They had changed the name so developers wouldn't assume it was the next version in line (and therefore better). But it could be compiled for both .NET and .NET Core. As a consequence, when you did a File-New Project-Web, you would have three very similar looking projects, ASP.NET .NET Framework, ASP.NET .NET Core (.NET Framework) and ASP.NET Core (.Net Core).

Two driving forces

As I see it, there were two major driving forces that led to what we later got to know as .NET Core.

First, there was an increasing need for cross-platform compatibility to stay relevant, and second, we had gotten to a place where we had too many subsets of the .NET framework, which was causing all sorts of problems as the subsets were created and maintained by different teams.

Figure 23 .NET Core was another attempt at true cross platform development

Since the first release in 2000, the .NET Framework has constantly evolved, but I think we can all agree that things started changing significantly after 2011. The trend towards cross-platform systems and applications couldn't be ignored, and as a result, JavaScript had a significant increase in popularity. Node.js came out for Linux and MacOS X, and we could write web applications, back and front, in JavaScript. Microsoft took notice and within the next decade changed the .NET web development forever.

> *Node.js*
>
> *Node.js is an open source, cross-platform runtime environment for developing server-side and networking applications. Node.js applications are written in JavaScript and can be run within the Node.js runtime on OS X, Microsoft Windows, and Linux.*

6

Modern Web Development

ASP.NET vs ASP.NET Core

ASP.NET Core was a complete rewrite. It was faster and modular, and everything was a NuGet package. It was host agnostic, had a light-weight HTTP pipeline, was cross platform, and you could deploy the application as a standalone package, with everything it needs and *only* what it needs.

The first versions of ASP.NET Core could on top of both the good old .NET Framework runtime (CLR), as well as on the .NET Core runtime (CoreCLR). In other words, developers could get the benefits from the rewrite without having to migrate everything to .NET Core. The alternative was to keep writing great applications in the original ASP.NET that hadn't been deprecated (but received less attention).

If you had the pleasure of following, maybe even experiencing first-hand, the first year or two with ASP.NET Core, you might have wished you had waited. There were many breaking changes and issues along the way. Most famously was the introduction of the project.json file that replaced the XML project file. Some were excited, some less so, but they had to go back on that decision, and today we are using csproj files again.

.NET Standard

I talked about the many subsets and forks of the .NET framework, and you might have noticed .NET Core doesn't solve the code sharing problem (at least not then or at the time of writing). In 2016, the .NET Standard was introduced as a way to bring everything together, and as something that would replace the Portable Class Libraries.

.NET Standard was a specification. It defined a set of available .NET APIs. You can think of it as interfaces and the frameworks that support the (or version of) .NET Standard as implementations. This is important to understand. It was a standard and not an actual implementation in contrast to the Portable Class Libraries that used a union model.

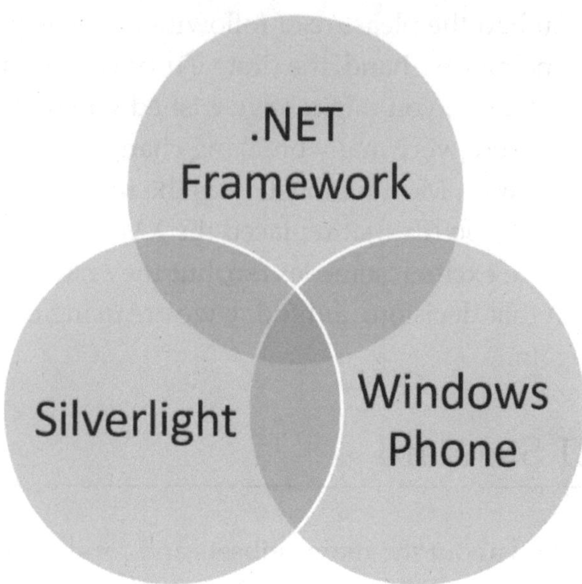

Figure 24 The union model meant only overlapping libraries could be used in the Portable Class Library. The intersection was referred to as the feature set.

What the target libraries had in common would be available in the PCL, which could be very little. And since you couldn't use conditional compilation in a PCL. For platform specific code you'd have to do some magic with the Adapter Pattern and Dependency Injection.

With .NET Standard every API was supported on every platform. And in addition, the .NET Standard was predictable because higher version meant more API coverage. If you wrote an open source library you would try to use the lowest possible version, and for consuming projects you'd often want to select the highest version to get as much coverage as possible.

You can explore the APIs here:
https://docs.microsoft.com/en-us/dotnet/api/

Razor Pages

We talked about the Razor syntax earlier, and to confuse developers even more, Razor pages was introduced. With .NET Core 2.0, a few changes to ASP.NET were introduced, one of them being Razor Pages.

This was a slimmer version of the MVC framework, an evolution of ASPX, and similar to the ASP.NET MVC view components. MVC, while a great pattern, introduced a new problem. Heavy controllers flocked with code. They became unreadable, and with that, difficult to maintain, unsecure, buggy, and a maintenance pain. The views, which were not supposed to contain business logic, ended up with it.

Razor Pages introduced a much-needed simplicity, where the pages were better scoped than the Controllers and Views would be. The idea was to put code only related to that page. Additionally, to highlight this point, the two files were tied together hierarchically in the IDEs, such as Visual Studio, which made it easier to find them compared to views and controllers that often had different names and locations.

Razor Pages example:

```
@page
@model IndexModel
@using Microsoft.AspNetCore.Mvc.RazorPages

@functions {
    public class IndexModel : PageModel
    {
        public string Message { get; private
set; } = "In page model: ";

        public void OnGet()
        {
            Message += $" Server seconds  {
DateTime.Now.Second.ToString() }";
        }
    }
}

<h2>In page sample</h2>
<p>
    @Model.Message
</p>
```

At this point, many of us thought this is it. ASP.NET Core, Razor Pages, .NET Core, .NET Standard. This was the future. However, Microsoft wanted to add something more to the future, Blazor.

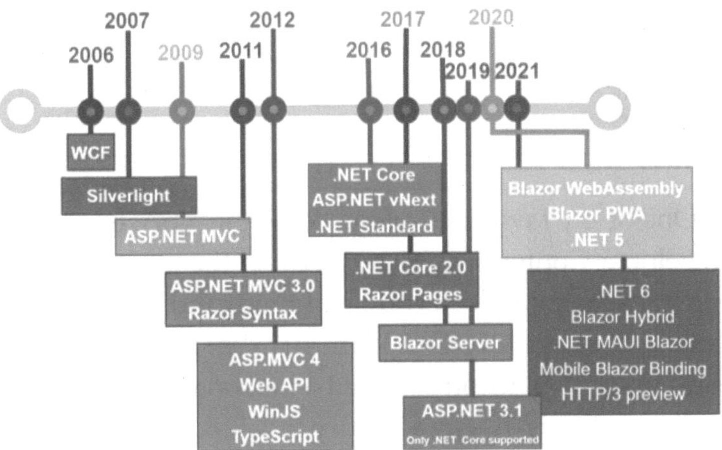

Figure 25 Modern and current .NET web development timeline. Full timeline can be found at the end of this book.

Blazor

One of my favorite conferences is the Norwegian Developer Conference, NDC. I've had the pleasure of being a speaker there a couple of times and an attendee as well. IT was at NDC Oslo in 2017 that Steve Sandersson, Microsoft, showed a personal project that blew our minds. It was a history breaking moment when Steve opened up Visual Studio and created a new project, MySuperThing, and casually showed how he could run C# and Razor in the browser using WebAssembly. WebAssembly is a specification for enabling the execution of binary code on the web. It brings languages other than HTML, CSS, and JavaScript to the browser. It was announced in 2015 and released in March 2017 as a joint effort to combine the power and security of an assembly-like language with the convenience of high-level languages. It was soon supported by all mainstream browsers, including on mobile devices.

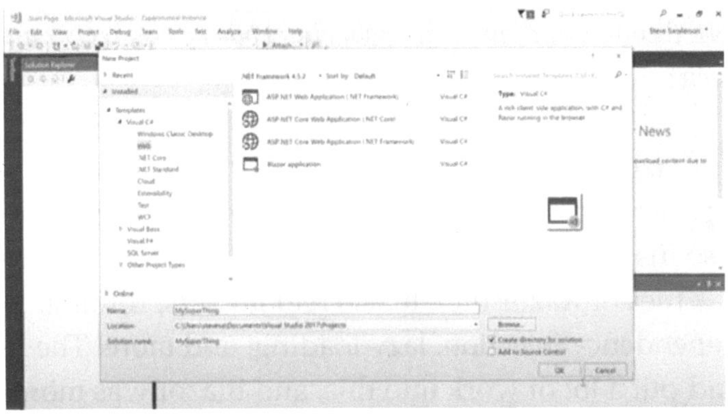

Figure 26 The moment that changed everything, Steve's super thing, Blazor

Sandersson was an early adopter and believer, and his project was adopted by Microsoft and rewritten from scratch by the ASP.NET team. The DotNetAnywhere repository had been inactive for a long time, and unsurprisingly, it was replaced by Mono, which had been acquired my Microsoft in 2016. In March 2018, the first public preview of Blazor was released.

> ***Quote, Steve Anderson's blog, Feb 6, 2018***
>
> *Today, the ASP.NET team announced that Blazor has moved into the ASP.NET organization, and we're beginning an experimental phase to see whether we can develop it into a supported shipping product. This is a big step forwards!*
>
> *What is Blazor? It's a framework for browser-based (client-side) applications written in .NET, running under WebAssembly. It gives you all the benefits of a rich, modern single-page application (SPA) platform while letting you use*

> *.NET end-to-end, including sharing code across server and client.*

Blazor was inspired by the top SPA (Single Page Applications) at the time: React, Vue, Angular. It was also inspired by Razor pages and was component based (C# files or Razor file). It also had layouts, routing, dependency injection, lazy loading, and more. The team had put a lot of work into this, and Blazor was more than an experimental project. Where did .NET Standard fit into this? Mono on WebAssembly supported netstandard2.0, even though not all the .NET APIs made sense in the browser.

Why *Blazor*?
Browser + Razor = Blazor.

Blazor was, from the start, compared to Silverlight. And while many were excited by the promise of being able to run C# in the browser, many were skeptical and predicted the death of Blazor within a year or two. Since the creation of .NET Silverlight, there had been a desire to have C# execute in a browser. It worked wonderfully for line-of-business apps, but the plug-in requirement was a problem. Blazor revived that dream of writing C# in the browser, and JavaScript interoperability for when C# wasn't enough. It started in the browser, but it didn't end there.

Mono

Microsoft Mono is a free and open-source software stack for building cross-platform applications. It includes a C# compiler and runtime, as well as a set of libraries for developing applications with a graphical user interface, database connectivity, and more. Mono is based on the .NET Framework, and it is compatible with Windows, macOS, Linux, and other operating systems. It was released in 2001, and it has since become one of the most popular options for developing cross-platform applications.

7

.NET Core no more

.NET Core Everywhere?

Was .NET Core, .NET Standard, and ASP.NET Core the future? Yes, and sort of no. .NET Core 3.0 (released on September 23, 2019) added support for WinForms and WPF (not cross-platform yet), and Microsoft made it clear that, moving forward, they highly recommended developers to target .NET Core, not .NET, which became even more obvious when ASP.NET Core 3.0 dropped support for compiling for .NET.

EF Core and Signalr Core

EF Core matured, there were tools for migrating, and Signalr Core (also a rewrite) came out of, and the library and tooling support for .NET Core exploded. Likewise, .NET Standard became a recognized and respected standard, and the majority of popular third-party libraries supported some version of it.

Entity Framework (EF)

EF was an open-source object-relational mapping tool for ADO.NET. It was first released with the .NET Framework. Entity Framework has been distributed separately from the .NET Framework since version 6. It was rewritten after .NET Core was released and rebranded.

EF Core was a cross-platform, open-source version of EF that could be used with various .NET implementations, including .NET Framework, .NET Core, and Mono. It included all the features of EF6 and new features, such as improved performance and a more modular design. Additionally, EF Core was much easier to port to different platforms than its predecessor. EF Core is a powerful ORM tool that offers many benefits over its predecessor.

Likewise, Signalr, was also rewritten. Signalr was a Microsoft ASP.NET library that allowed developers to add real-time web functionality to their applications. It made it easy to add real-time features, like chat, collaboration, and gaming to web applications. Signalr used websockets under the hood, but it also supported other transport methods for older browsers.

Signalr Core was a new implementation with significant differences from the original Signalr with limited parity. Nonetheless, it was an improvement and highlighted Microsoft's move away from different implementations when they let developers know that Signalr Core was the future.

And then bam, the announcement we had all anticipated. .NET Framework 4.8 would be the last major version of .NET Framework. But what did that mean?

.NET Core No More

In November 2020, Microsoft released .NET 5.0 and left many scratching their heads. If .NET Framework 4.8 was the last major version, then what is this? At the same time, Core was no more. Microsoft had dropped the "Core" branding, skipping .NET Core 4 (to avoid conflation with the .NET Framework), and instead named the version .NET 5, the only .NET framework moving forward.

".NET 5.0 is the first release in our .NET unification journey. We built .NET 5.0 to enable a much larger group of developers to migrate their .NET Framework code and apps to .NET 5.0. We've also done much of the early work in 5.0, so Xamarin developers can use the unified .NET platform when we release .NET 6.0. There is more on .NET unification later, in the post." – Microsoft DevBlogs

NET 5 key features included:

- A single unified platform

- including Windows, Mac, Web, Mobile, Cloud, IoT, Gaming, Machine Learning and Data Science.
- Open source (and supported by Microsoft)
- Cross-platform
- Supports all major platform capabilities for .NET Framework, .NET Core and Xamarin including Windows Forms, WPF, UWP, ASP.NET MVC, Entity Framework, LINQ and so on.
- Scalable, fast, and high performance
- Smaller deployment and packages
- Support of the most productive IDEs and tools including Visual Studio, VS Code, VS for Mac, and Command Line Interface (CLI)

There are two runtimes of interest, Mono and CoreCLR. Mono is the runtime used as a part of Xamarin and is used to build cross-platform applications. CoreCLR is the runtime used as a part of .NET Core. .NET 5 supports both and will continue to do so.

What about .NET Standard

When .NET was released, developers were quick to ask what would happen to the .NET Standard now that .NET 5 was cross-platform (this time for real).

So, what about .NET Standard?

.NET 5 makes .NET Standard obsolete in the future. Why not now?

Because it takes time for libraries, apps, and systems to catch up. Therefore, Microsoft promised all future versions will continue to support .NET Standard 2.1 and earlier, but moving forward, .NET 5 is the way to go to share code across platform and devices.

The general guidelines, as a response to this, were (and to a degree still are at the time of writing):

- Use netstandard2.0 to share code between .NET Framework and all other platforms.
- Use netstandard2.1 to share code between Mono, Xamarin, and .NET Core 3.x.
- Use net5.0 for code sharing moving forward.

This was reflected in the target framework names:

net5.0: cross platform. Core and .NET Standard combined and replaces the netcoreapp and netstandard target framework names.

net5.0-windows (and net6.0-android, net6.0-ios): operating system specific.

8

Current Web Development

ASP.NET Core

.NET Core 3.0 and 3.1 (which included ASP.NET Core 3.0 and 3.1) were released only a few months apart. As mentioned earlier, ASP.NET Core 3.0 surprised many by dropping support for .NET Framework and thus only supporting .NET Core (and .NET Standard). The next version, 3.1 didn't introduce many breaking changes, nor significant architectural changes. Besides the usual performance improvement, there was a change to the behavior of SameSite cookies in ASP.NET Core (because of a new standard proposed by Google), and a long list of Windows Forms controls weren't available anymore.

SameSite

Cookies with the same-site attribute were a 2016 draft standard extension to HTTP. It intended to protect against Cross-Site Request Forgery (CSRF) and was originally intended as a server option that the new parameters would enable. However, Google issued a new draft standard that isn't backwards compatible. The default mode is changed to Lax, and a new entry None is added to opt out from the norm. For most app cookies, lax suffices; nevertheless, it fails cross-site situations such as OpenID Connect and WS-Federation login.

The replacement controls had been around for a while, but Windows Forms controls hadn't been removed. Some controls were: DataGrid*, Menu*, Toolbar*, and GridTables*. However, there were many changes related to Razor and Blazor, and this sent an obvious message regarding the future of Blazor. Blazor was not an experiment anymore. We will cover Blazor changes in a separate section.

With ASP.NET Core for .NET 5 (notice that the change in name) performance was further improved, and so were model bindings. For example, they now supported C# 9 record types. OpenAPI and Swagger UI were added, Signalr hub filters and parallel invocations, HTTP/2 and gRPC performance enhancements. See the note section for more.

C# 9 record types

C# record types are immutable data structures that contain a set of named fields. The fields of a record can be of any type, including other record types. Records are declared using the keyword record, followed by the name of the record and the list of fields.

ASP.NET Core for .NET 6 was packed with improvements and new features, including for Blazor. Some significant changes were: hot reload for Razor, minimal APIs, async streaming, null-state analysis (on by default), JavaScript modules, HTTP/3 (Preview): and more. Se note section for more.

Hot reload

Let's you apply changes to Razor, C#, and CSS source files in a running app during development without the need to rebuild and restart the app.

New in ASP.NET Core 3.1

Partial class support for Razor components
Pass parameters to top-level components
Component tag helper
Prevent default actions for events (Blazor apps)
Stop event propagation (Blazor apps)
Detailed errors during development (Blazor app)
Support for shared queues in HttpSysServer

New in ASP.NET Core for .NET 5

MVC model binding improvements, including support for C# 9 record types
Blazor Server & Blazor WebAssembly support and improvements
Built-in OpenAPI and Swagger UI support for Web APIs
SignalR Hub filters and parallel Hub invocations
Azure AD authentication with Microsoft.Identity.Web
Auto browser refresh with dotnet watch
HTTP/2 and gRPC performance improvements
Source: https://devblogs.microsoft.com/dotnet/announcing-asp-net-core-in-net-5

New in ASP.NET Core for .NET 6

Hot reload
Minimal APIs
Async streaming
IAsyncDisposable
Bootstrap 5.1
Null-state analysis
CSS isolation for pages and views
JavaScript modules
.NET WebAssembly build tools
Single-page apps
Socket control
Strongly-typed headers
HTTP & W3C logging
HTTP/3 (Preview)
See Blazor section below for list of Blazor features released with .NET 6.

Blazor: Server and WebAssembly

Blazor was made a part of .NET Core with the 3.0 version, and from there on Blazor versions were aligned with the .NET Core versions. In 2019 when Blazor had its first official preview, the version was 3.0.0-previewX, and not 0.X. Personally, I was thrilled about that, as it's difficult to keep track of versions and align them, unless bundled. However, Blazor was more than just 'one' Blazor. Blazor had and has different hosting models.

Blazor server (also referred to as Server-side Blazor) Blazor server was previously named ASP.NET Razor Components). It is hosted on ASP.NET and has a thin client. The Blazor components run on the server and UI events that occur in the browser are sent to the server.

Blazor WebAssembly (also referred to as Client-side Blazor)

Single-Page-Apps run on the user's browser (downloaded to the browser). In other words, the apps execute directly in the browser on a WebAssembly-based .NET runtime.

Blazor Server shipped with .NET Core 3.0, while Blazor WebAssembly was still in preview but no experimental considered experimental. A year later, in 2020, with .NET 3.2, Blazor WebAssembly was finally officially released, with support for Progressive Web Apps.

Blazor Progressive Web Apps (PWA)

Blazor Progressive Web Apps (PWAs) are web apps that are built using the Blazor framework and can be deployed to any static web hosting service. Blazor PWAs take advantage of many modern web features, including service workers, IndexedDB, and push notifications, to provide a user experience similar to that of native apps. Additionally, Blazor PWAs can be installed on devices just like any other app, allowing users to access them offline and receive push notifications even when the browser is not open. Overall, Blazor PWAs provide a way to build rich, interactive web apps that can take advantage of many of the same features as native apps.

Figure 27 PWA Logo by Maxim Salnikov.

Progressive web apps (PWAs) are type of apps that offer an immersive, app-like experience on a web platform. Unlike traditional web apps, PWAs can be installed on devices and accessed offline. In addition, they offer many of the same features as native apps, such as push notifications and camera access. While PWAs are still in their early stages, they have already gained traction with major brands, such as Twitter and Pinterest. Moreover, they offer several advantages over traditional web apps and native apps. For example, PWAs are easier to develop and deploy, and they are more compatible with all types of devices. In addition, PWAs are more discoverable than traditional web apps and offer a better user experience. As a result, it is likely that PWAs will continue to gain popularity in the years to come, and Microsoft is spot on with their support for PWA.

With .NET 6 Microsoft added two more Blazor hosting models to the mix, one experimental, Blazor Hybrid, and one in the very early planning stages, Blazor Native.

Blazor improvements with .NET 6 (and ASP.NET Core for .NET 6)

Preserve pre-rendered state
Error boundaries
Custom event args
Infer generic type parameters from ancestor components

> *Required component parameters*
> *Handle query string parameters*
> *Control HTML head content*
> *JavaScript initializers*
> *Dynamically render components*

Blazor Hybrid and Blazor Native

Blazor Hybrid, and Native, are extensions of Blazor that use the same Blazor technology as Blazor Server and Blazor WebAssembly. The hosting models are built on .NET 6 and .NET MAUI and lets you build cross-platform native apps, with full native device access.

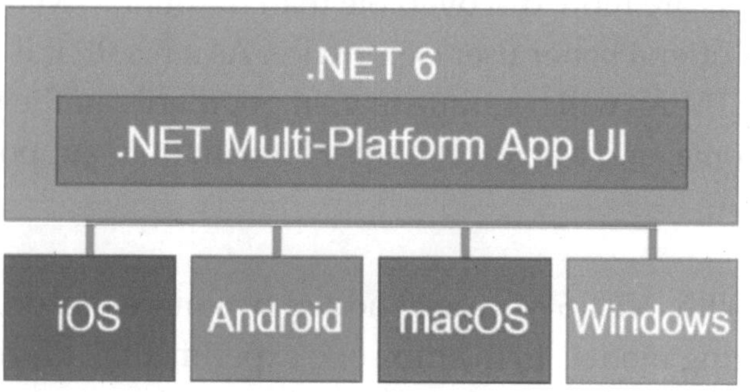

Figure 28 .MAUI

Additionally, you can use your existing Razor Class Libraries (RCLs). These apps can run on Windows, macOS, Android, iOS. The app runs 100% natively in one process. In other words, no HTTP, no browser sandbox, no network. The hybrid model means there is a HTML UI rendered into a WebView control, but the code runs locally. The WebView is the only web app similarity there is for the hybrid model. However, with Mobile Blazor Bindings (MBB), you can build native apps.

> ***Mobile Blazor Bindings (MBB)***
>
> *MBB is a new Microsoft technology announced in 2020, that allows developers to build native mobile apps using C# and .NET. MBB apps are built using the same WebAssembly-based framework as traditional Blazor apps, but they also include bindings for native mobile controls and services. This makes it possible to write entire app sections in C#, while still taking advantage of the native performance and user experience of each platform.*

> ***.NET MAUI***
>
> *MAUI is the .NET Multi-platform App UI, a new framework that enables developers to build native mobile apps for iOS, Android, and Windows from a single codebase. .NET MAUI is built on top of the existing Xamarin.Forms framework, making it easy for developers to get started with MAUI without having to learn a new platform. .NET MAUI also includes a number of new features that improve performance and enable collaboration between developers working on different platforms. In addition, MAUI takes advantage of the latest improvements in .NET 5, which enables developers to take advantage of mobile hardware capabilities such as cameras and sensors. With MAUI, developers can build cross-platform mobile apps that are fast, responsive, and provide a consistent user experience across all devices.*

Razor Class Libraries (RCLs)

Razor Class libraries (released with ASP.NET Core 2.1) were created to bundle and distribute UI components that may be utilized and consumed in a host application. They are a set of libraries that allow developers to share code across multiple applications. RCLs are compiled into a single assembly, which can then be referenced by any number of applications. This allows for consistent behavior and implementation across all applications that use the RCL. Razor Class Libraries also support versioning, so that different versions of an RCL can be used by different applications. This allows for greater flexibility when upgrading or deploying new applications.

.NET MAUI Blazor VS Mobile Blazor Binding

At the time of writing, Blazor MAUI only supports the hybrid model I described earlier. This is because the mobile bindings are still considered experimental. Blazor MAUI renders everything into a WebView, while the mobile bindings are using Xamarin.Forms components (this will most likely change).

As the web continues to evolve, so does the need for more powerful and interactive web applications. Flash and Silverlight were once seen as the future of web development, but they have since fallen out of favor due to their poor performance and security vulnerabilities. HTML5 and JavaScript have emerged as the new gold standard for web development, but they still have limitations. While still in its early stages, Blazor has the potential to revolutionize web development by providing a more powerful and performant alternative to HTML5 and JavaScript. In the coming years, we can expect to see more and more developers adopt Blazor as their go-to framework for building modern (web) applications.

9

The Future

When I wrote the rough draft for this book, this was one section that seemed obvious to include. The future of .NET web development. It sounded good. It sounded like a good way to wrap up the book. After all, I had seen this layout in many of the book I had read that covered the history of ...something. However, as I got to the end and current times, I realized two things:

One, it's hard to foresee what will happen as the evolution of technologies is fast paced with many moving and unpredictable parts. The pandemic, Covid-19, is a perfect example. It sped up the adoption of already planned cloud applications, services and infrastructure by 53% (Harvard Business Review Analytic Services Survey, September 2020).

Second, unless I try to look ahead at least five years, it will probably be too late by the time the book is in your hands. So instead of making educated guesses that will probably be inaccurate, I've decided to focus on the past and how we got to where we are today. And to be honest, it's much more gratifying to see the impact that ASP.NET has had on web development in the past than to speculate on what might happen in the future.

Thirdly, because off-by-one is the most common mistake developers do, I'm worried I'll disclose something I'm not supposed to share. NDA's and all that jazz.

So instead of writing about the future of .NET web development, I want to share some of my thoughts on where I think web development is heading in general.

The web has come a long way in the past 20 years. In the early days, the web was mostly static content with a few basic interactions. Over time, we've seen the addition of dynamic content, streaming media, real-time communications, and much more. The trend seems to be toward more immersive and interactive experiences.

We're also seeing the web become more ubiquitous. It's not just on our desktops and laptops anymore. We now have web-connected TVs, game consoles, cars, and even appliances. The internet of things is upon us and the web will be a central part of that.

The trend toward more immersive and interactive experiences will continue. We'll see more use of virtual reality and augmented reality. We'll see more use of voice and natural language interfaces. And we'll see more AI-powered assistants, and AI added to everyday applications. Unfortunately, both ethical and unethical AI.

The web will also become more distributed. The traditional three-tier architecture of web applications (client, server, and database) will give way to a more distributed architecture, with the browser becoming just one of many clients. You'd think this was already the case, but probably only because we talk a lot about it. Some things take time to change, in particular old-school systems that are either too fragile or too sturdy to be rewritten without significant cost.

As I mentioned earlier, cloud adoption was heavily affected by the pandemic, and even with the unexpected world situation and consequentially increased cloud adoptions, there are still many companies that aren't mature enough or have legislative obstacles (in particular the public sector).

Azure, *AWS* and *Google Cloud Platform* lead the pack of public cloud providers.

Public cloud provider adoption rates for all organizations

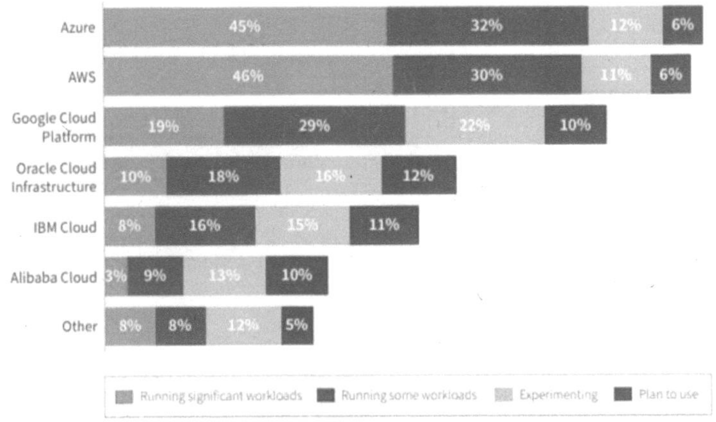

Source: Flexera 2022 State of the Cloud Report

Flexera

Cost-control measures and moving to SaaS solutions are top of mind.

Top cloud initiatives for 2022 across all organizations

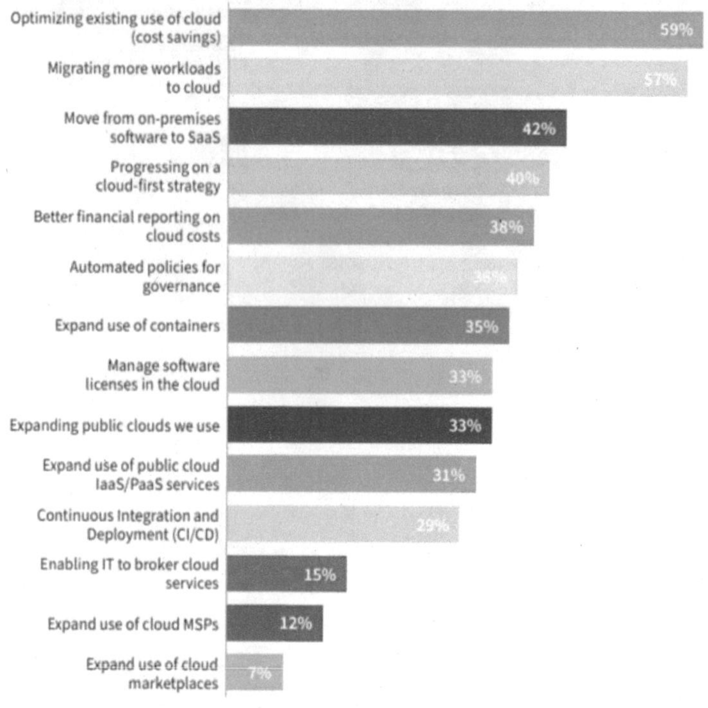

N=753
Source, Flexera 2022 State of the Cloud Report
Flexera

> ***Six levels of cloud maturity (source: New Relic)***
>
> *Experimenting: What is the cloud?*
> *Securing the cloud: Can we trust the cloud?*
> *Enabling servers and SaaS: Lift-and-shift, confirmation the cloud works pretty well*
> *Enabling value added services: Dynamic cloud becomes a practice*
> *Enabling unique services: Dynamic cloud is deeply ingrained in the culture*
> *Mandating cloud usage: Why do we need our own data centers?*

This means the move towards the cloud will continue, maybe even accelerate. Web applications will make use of cloud services and be built on top of microservices' architectures. This will result in a more distributed, and therefore more complex, web.

We'll also see more use of serverless architectures. These are event-driven architectures that make use of managed services provided by cloud providers. They're well suited for applications that are highly scalable and have bursty usage patterns. And we'll see more use of containers. These are lightweight, isolated environments that make it easy to deploy and run applications in the cloud.

Finally, we'll see the web become more open. The days of closed, proprietary standards are numbered.

The web will continue to be built on open standards and technologies.

These are just a few of the trends that I see shaping the future of web development. It's an exciting time to be a web developer and I can't wait to see what the next 20 years bring.

What do you think? What trends do you see shaping the future of web development? And where does the ecosystem of .NET web development fit into all of this?

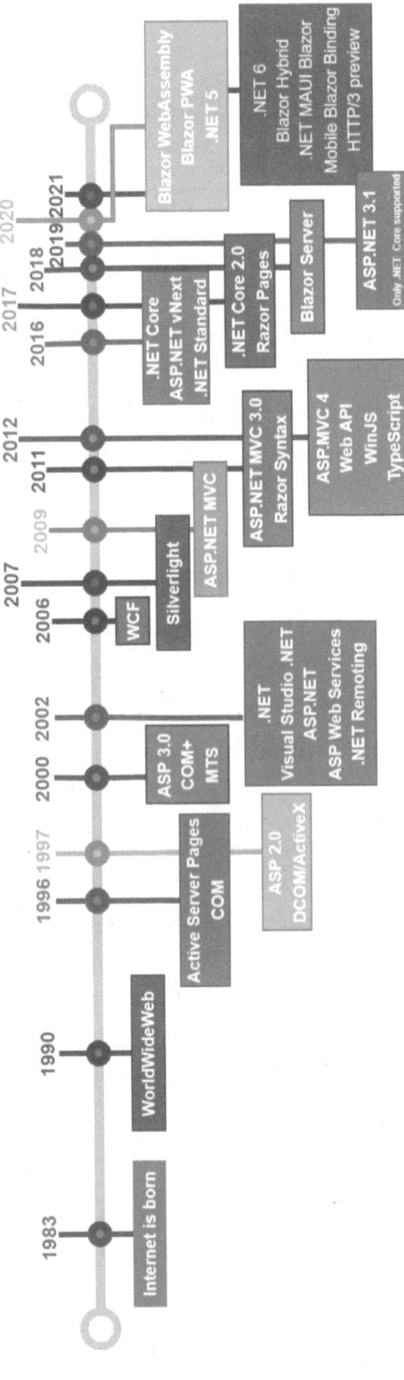
1983
Internet is born
1990
WorldWideWeb
1996
Active Server Pages
COM
1997
ASP 2.0
DCOM/ActiveX
2000
ASP 3.0
COM+
MTS
2002
.NET
Visual Studio .NET
ASP.NET
ASP Web Services
.NET Remoting
2006
WCF
2007
Silverlight
2009
ASP.NET MVC
2011
ASP.NET MVC 3.0
Razor Syntax
2012
ASP.MVC 4
Web API
WinJS
TypeScript
2016
.NET Core
ASP.NET vNext
.NET Standard
2017
.NET Core 2.0
Razor Pages
2018
Blazor Server
2019
ASP.NET 3.1
Only .NET Core supported
2020
Blazor WebAssembly
Blazor PWA
.NET 5
2021
.NET 6
Blazor Hybrid
.NET MAUI Blazor
Mobile Blazor Binding
HTTP/3 preview

Staying up to date

I do a lot of speaking at conferences and schools, and a reoccurring question I get is 'How do I stay up to date?'. Reading books like this is a great starting point, but they might not always be up to date (although I'll do my best!). The web is a great place to start, and I'm going to share some of my favorite sources for .NET news.

Official blogs

First up is the official .NET blog, which is run by the .NET product team. This is a great place to stay up to date on all things .NET, from new releases and features, to previews and beta versions. There are different categories, but the dotnet blog posts is a great start: https://devblogs.microsoft.com/dotnet

Community blogs

Besides the .NET blog, there are various other blogs written by Microsoft MVPs (Most Valuable Professionals) and other community leaders. These can be found all over the internet, but a great starting place is the ASP.NET Community blog: https://www.asp.net/community/blogs

This blog contains a collection of articles from a variety of different authors, all writing about ASP.NET and web development. If you're looking for something specific, there's a good chance you'll find it here. I have a blog, irisclasson.com, but I write about different things related to programming, not just the latest news.

Social media: Twitter

Another way to stay up to date is through social media. Twitter is a great platform for following people in the .NET community and seeing what they're talking about. I would recommend following the official .NET account, as well as some of the more popular community leaders. Here are a few to get you started:

.NET - https://twitter.com/dotnet

ASP.NET - https://twitter.com/aspnet

Scott Hanselman - https://twitter.com/shanselman

Phil Haack - https://twitter.com/haacked

Iris Classon - https://twitter.com/irisclasson

Social media: YouTube

And finally, don't forget about YouTube! There are a lot of great channels out there with all kinds of content, from conference talks to screencasts and educational videos. A few of my favorites are:

.NET Conf - https://www.youtube.com/channel/UCMh-ezZ7zsLs4C4In9Jwi3w

Microsoft Visual Studio - https://www.youtube.com/user/VisualStudio

DotNetRocks - https://www.youtube.com/channel

Microsoft Developer - https://www.youtube.com/user/microsoftdeveloper

DotNetConf - https://www.youtube.com/channel/UCrlY7T4JfIwFpgAi905zvHQ

MS Dev Show - https://www.youtube.com/channel/UCsMica-v34IrX1fcH2rjJxQ

Conferences: Attending

Another great way to stay up to date is to attend conferences. Some conferences are also completely free to attend virtually such as .NET Conf. Here are some of the bigger conferences:

Build - https://www.microsoft.com/en-us/build

Ignite - https://www.microsoft.com/ignite

Connect(); - https://connectevent.visualstudio.com

NDCConferences - https://ndcsydney.com https://ndcoslo.com

Conferences: Watch recorded sessions or attend virtually

Conferences such as those listed above can be really pricey, but fortunately, they almost always post the recorded sessions for free online. You can usually find them on the conference website or on YouTube. Additionally, a lot of conferences now offer the option to attend virtually for free. This is a great way to get all the benefits of attending without having to pay for a ticket or travel.

Dotnet conf: https://github.com/dotnet-presentations/dotNETConf

Build: https://mybuild.microsoft.com/en-US/archives

NDC: https://www.youtube.com/c/NDCConferences

Online education platforms

Microsoft Learn is a free, online education platform that includes interactive modules, hands-on labs, and videos. It provides a personalized learning experience that adapts to your level of expertise and helps you build the skills you need to be successful with Microsoft technologies. Whether you're just getting started or you're a seasoned pro, Microsoft Learn can help you grow your skills.

https://docs.microsoft.com/en-us/learn

Other popular platforms are:

Pluralsight: https://www.pluralsight.com/courses

Udemy: https://udemy.com

Documentation

This one should probably be further up on the list, but I put here as documentation is a place you usually go to when you are looking for something specific, not necessarily to stay up to date. You can however watch the repository, but more about that later.

The Microsoft Docs website also includes a variety of different resources, such as articles, tutorials, and code samples. This is a great place to go if you're looking for specific information about a certain topic.

https://docs.microsoft.com

GitHub repositories

GitHub is a great place to find open-source projects, and a lot of times the repositories will include documentation or other resources that can be helpful. You can also watch repositories, which means you'll get notified whenever there's a new commit (change). This can be a great way to stay up to date on what's happening with a certain project, and you can even filter the notifications, so you only see the ones that are relevant to you. Microsoft has many repositories that might be of interest, in particular:

.NET: https://github.com/dotnet

Visual Studio: https://github.com/MicrosoftDocs/visualstudio-docs

Windows: https://github.com/MicrosoftDocs/windows

Tools & Libraries: https://github.com/microsoft/vscode

ASP.NET: https://github.com/aspnet

Entity Framework: https://github.com/aspnet/EntityFrameworkCore

Xamarin: https://github.com/xamarin

There are many other repositories, these are just some of the more popular ones. You can find a complete list here: https://opensource.microsoft

Afterword

I've tried hard to squeeze in, in a dense version, everything that has happened while trying to make it easy to understand and follow.

I don't think I've succeeded as well as I had hoped. Nonetheless, I hope this has been a decent recap and introduction. When I was learning programming, there weren't any books like this out there, and I wish there had been.

This is a field that changes, and changes fast. Don't panic if you feel out of the loop. Embrace what you already know and embrace the changes to come.

I will continue writing these types of books and keep this one up to date (yearly update), and hopefully that will help new developers, as well as veterans, stay up to date and provide some background on how we ended up here.

Thank you for reading. Please contact me if something is missing. Reviews are always welcome.

ABOUT THE AUTHOR

Iris Classon

Software Developer, Author, Microsoft MVP, Sporty Spice wannabe

Iris Classon is an appreciated speaker, author, Microsoft C# MVP, and Pluralsight trainer with a tremendous passion for programming. She has had a remarkable career path that proves nothing is impossible. Switching from a licensed and registered clinical dietician to a software developer with a dozen certifications, applications, books, and jobs with renowned companies.

She has been featured in several newspaper articles, online articles, and podcasts, such as Hanselminutes, Computer Sweden, and Developer Magazine. As a sought-after and frequent speaker at conferences, such as TechDays, NDC, and various user groups, she is known for her unique, creative, and uplifting presentation style.

After bragging for half a page, she would like to say she finds the bio a tad embarrassing, but an American friend wrote it, and he says it'll help her sell more books.

Other books by Iris

The Unlikely Success of a Copy-Paste Developer
Genre: Comedic Fiction
Where: https://thecopypastedeveloper.com
Format: Hardcover, paperback, eBook

A Copy-Paste Developer is Born (a prequel)
Release date June/July 2022
Genre: Comedic Fiction

Where: https://thecopypastedeveloper.com
Format: Hardcover, paperback, eBook

Programming Windows Store Apps
Genre: Technical
Format: Paperback, eBook

Migrating to ASP.NET Core
Genre: Technical
Format: Paperback, eBook

Azure on a Shoestring
Genre: Technical
Format: eBook

Loose Candy: Pick and Mix Power Tips for .NET Developers and IT Professionals
Genre: Technical
Format: eBook

www.ingramcontent.com/pod-product-compliance
Ingram Content Group UK Ltd.
Pitfield, Milton Keynes, MK11 3LW, UK
UKHW012253290726
14090UKWH00016B/615

9 789198 778359